Designed by Flowerpot Press
www.FlowerpotPress.com
CHC-0909-0501
ISBN: 978-1-4867-1850-4
Made in China/Fabriqué en Chine

Rectangular Prism

HOW DO YOU MEASURE A SLICE OF PIZZA?
A BOOK ABOUT GEOMETRY

PERFECT SLICE!

CHOCOLATE

VANILLA

DARK CHOCOLATE

LEMON

written by madeline j. hayes
and lucy d. hayes
illustrated by srimalie bassani

Clifton Park - Halfmoon Public Library
475 Moe Road
Clifton Park, NY 12065

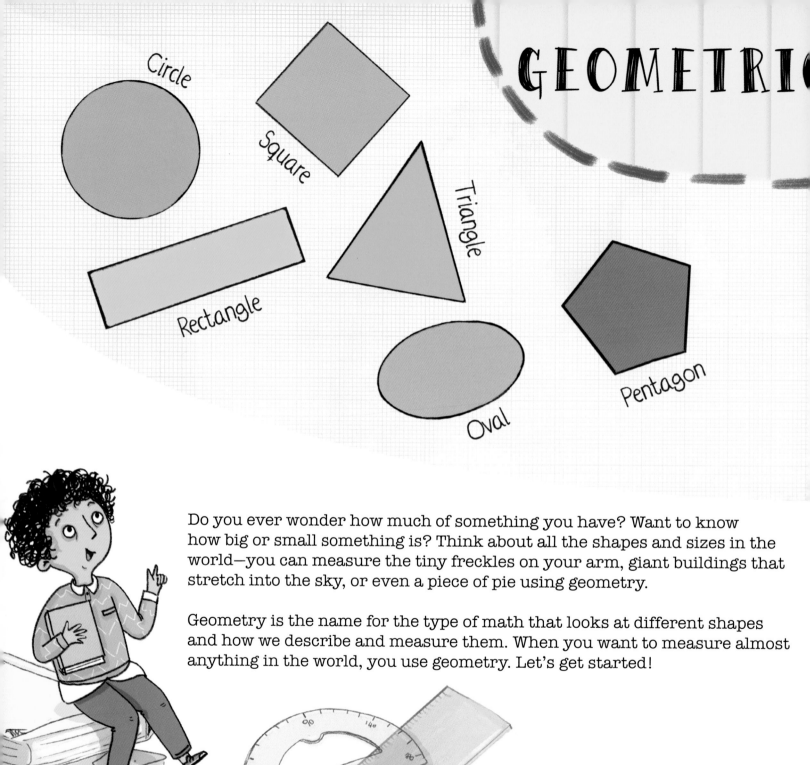

Circle

Square

Triangle

Rectangle

Pentagon

Oval

Do you ever wonder how much of something you have? Want to know how big or small something is? Think about all the shapes and sizes in the world—you can measure the tiny freckles on your arm, giant buildings that stretch into the sky, or even a piece of pie using geometry.

Geometry is the name for the type of math that looks at different shapes and how we describe and measure them. When you want to measure almost anything in the world, you use geometry. Let's get started!

SHAPES

Rectangular Prism

Cylinder

Cone

Sphere

Cube

Pyramid

Too small!

Purrfect prism!

How do you measure a pizza box?
Do you see how many small boxes you can fit into one big box?

Fit boxes inside another box?!?! I guess that's one way to do it!

You can also just measure the box to find its area. Since pizza boxes come in all shapes and sizes, first decide what shape your box is. If all four sides of the box are the same length, you have a square. If two of the sides are longer than the other two sides, you have a rectangle.

To practice finding the area of a pizza box, you can measure this teeny, tiny box!

To find the area of a square or a rectangle, you measure how long one side of the box is and call that the length.

length = 4 cm

width = 4 cm

Then you measure how long the side perpendicular to the length is and call that the width.

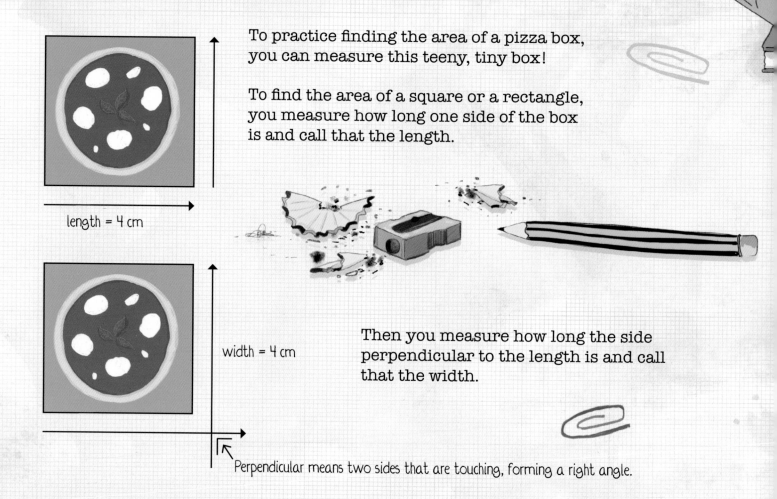

Perpendicular means two sides that are touching, forming a right angle.

Once you have determined the length and the width, you multiply them to get the area of the pizza box.

width = 4 cm

length = 4 cm

Area of a Square or Rectangle

Formula:
Area = length x width

Equation:
Area = 4 cm x 4 cm

Answer:
Area = 16 cm²

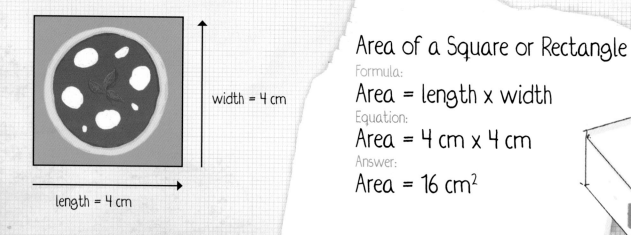

I have an extra large pizza!

The length and width of my pizza box are equal so I have a square.

When you multiply two units together, you have to use a new unit to describe something that goes in two directions, instead of just one. The unit you use is called a squared unit.

If you multiply the length and width of a square that is measured in cm, you also multiply the units.

$$cm \times cm = cm^2$$

The little two means the unit is squared. You use squared units when you are trying to describe an area!

How do you measure a pizza?
Do you eat it all and see how full you get?

pineapple

chili pepper

basil

ham

mozzarella

shrimp

cheese

onion

mushrooms

Eat all the pizza?!?! No way!

To measure a pizza, you will need to know how to measure the area of a circle. We use a special number called Pi to measure circles. This Pi isn't the delicious kind of pie you eat, it's actually a special number that goes on for a REALLY long time. Usually it is shortened to 3.14 and is represented by this symbol: π.

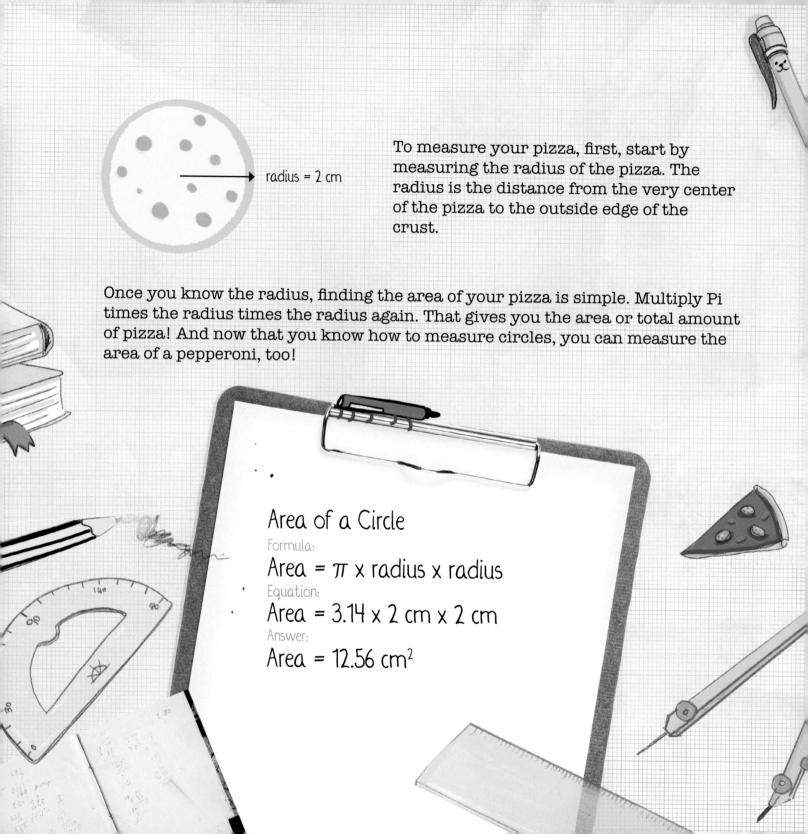

radius = 2 cm

To measure your pizza, first, start by measuring the radius of the pizza. The radius is the distance from the very center of the pizza to the outside edge of the crust.

Once you know the radius, finding the area of your pizza is simple. Multiply Pi times the radius times the radius again. That gives you the area or total amount of pizza! And now that you know how to measure circles, you can measure the area of a pepperoni, too!

Area of a Circle
Formula:
Area = π x radius x radius
Equation:
Area = 3.14 x 2 cm x 2 cm
Answer:
Area = 12.56 cm²

Helpful Hint: Sometimes finding the very center of your pizza isn't easy, so another option is to measure the diameter of your pizza. The diameter is the length from the outside edge of the crust all the way across the pizza to the outside edge of the crust on the other side. Once you know the diameter, you can just divide the diameter by two to get the radius.

Radius of a Circle

Formula:

$$\text{Radius} = \frac{\text{diameter}}{2}$$

Equation:

$$\text{Radius} = \frac{4\ \text{cm}}{2}$$

Answer:

$$\text{Radius} = 2\ \text{cm}$$

How do you measure a slice of pizza?
Do you toss it onto your brother's head to see if it is bigger?

Hey!

Use your brother's head?!?! No way!
All the toppings might fall off!

You can measure a slice of pizza by finding its area.
When you slice up a pizza, you get a new shape to
measure—a triangle! A slice of pizza isn't actually a
perfect triangle, because the crust doesn't have a straight
base. To get an easier measurement, just cut off the crust.

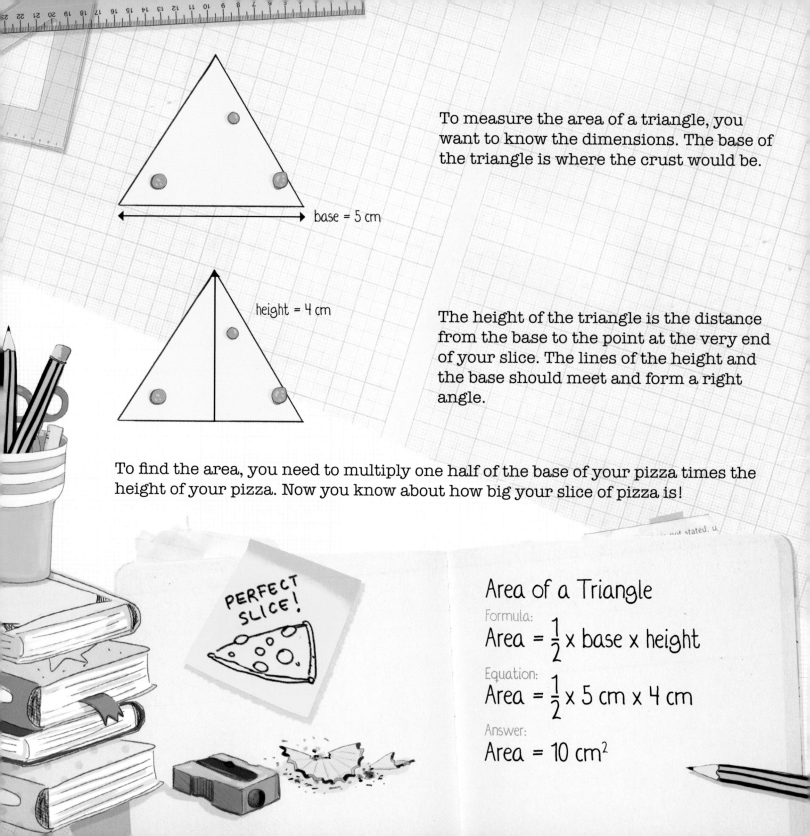

base = 5 cm

To measure the area of a triangle, you want to know the dimensions. The base of the triangle is where the crust would be.

height = 4 cm

The height of the triangle is the distance from the base to the point at the very end of your slice. The lines of the height and the base should meet and form a right angle.

To find the area, you need to multiply one half of the base of your pizza times the height of your pizza. Now you know about how big your slice of pizza is!

PERFECT SLICE!

Area of a Triangle

Formula:

$$Area = \frac{1}{2} \times base \times height$$

Equation:

$$Area = \frac{1}{2} \times 5 \text{ cm} \times 4 \text{ cm}$$

Answer:

$$Area = 10 \text{ cm}^2$$

How do you measure an ice-cream cone?
Do you fill it up with pudding and see how much it holds?

A pudding cone?!?! No way!

It's important to know how big your cone is so you know how much room you have for ice cream! A cone is basically just a triangle spun all the way around in a circle. A cone is not flat like a triangle or a circle, so we call it a three-dimensional shape. A three-dimensional shape is a shape that you measure in three directions—height, width, and length.

When measuring a three-dimensional shape, you want to measure the volume instead of the area to know how much it can hold.

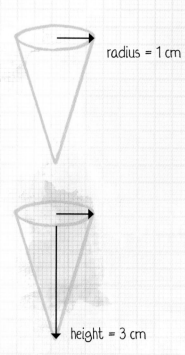

radius = 1 cm

To find the volume of a cone, first you look at the circle on the end (the place where you put the ice cream) and find its area. To find its area, use the formula for circles (Pi x radius x radius).

height = 3 cm

Then multiply the area of the circle (the base of the cone) by $\frac{1}{3}$ and then multiply that by the height of the cone. Now you know how much ice cream your cone can hold.

Volume of a Cone

Formula:

Volume = π x radius x radius x $\frac{1}{3}$ x height

Equation:

Volume = 3.14 x 1 cm x 1 cm x $\frac{1}{3}$ x 3 cm

Answer:

Volume = 3.14 cm^3

Difference between a 2D shape and a 3D shape

height

width

2D shapes only have two dimensions

height

width

length

3D shapes have three dimensions

When we look at volume we don't just look at the triangle shape on the side of the cone or the circle shape at the end— we look at the whole thing.

CHOCOLATE

VANILLA

Two cones with extra room for ice cream, please!

When you multiply three units together, you have to use a new unit to describe something that goes in three directions, instead of just one or two. This unit is called a cubed unit. If you multiply the height, length, and width of a cube that is measured in cm, you also multiply the units.

cm x cm x cm = cm^3

The little three means the unit is cubed. You used cubed units when you are trying to describe a volume!

How do you measure a scoop of ice cream?
Do you put it on your bathroom scale and see how much it weighs?

Feet-flavored ice cream?!?! No way!

To measure the perfect scoop of ice cream, you just need to know the volume of a sphere. A sphere is a three-dimensional shape that looks like a perfectly round scoop of ice cream. A perfect sphere has the same height, width, and depth all the way around.

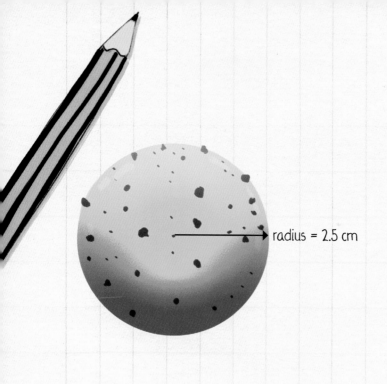

radius = 2.5 cm

Pretend your ice cream is a perfect sphere. To figure out the volume, you first need to find the radius.

Once you have the radius, you multiply it by itself three times. Then multiply that value by $\frac{4}{3}$ times Pi. Then you will know how much ice cream you have in your cone!

Volume of a Sphere

Formula:

$$\text{Volume} = \text{radius} \times \text{radius} \times \text{radius} \times \frac{4}{3} \times \pi$$

Equation:

$$\text{Volume} = 2.5 \text{ cm} \times 2.5 \text{ cm} \times 2.5 \text{ cm} \times \frac{4}{3} \times 3.14$$

Answer:

$$\text{Volume} = 65.45 \text{ cm}^3$$

Helpful Hint: If you cut a sphere in half, you will find that the shape inside is a circle. This means a sphere has a radius just like a circle. To find the radius of a sphere, you can either measure from the middle to the edge OR measure all the way across the sphere to get the diameter and then divide the diameter by two. You can use the radius of a circle formula you have already learned.

diameter = 5 cm

sphere

cone

shapes

How do you measure an entire ice-cream cone?
Do you see how far you can throw it?

Throw ice cream?!?! No way!

To measure the entire ice-cream cone, you can use
a lot of things you've already learned.

sphere

cone

+

=

ice cream with 1 scoop

$$r \times r \times r \times \frac{4}{3} \times \pi \quad + \quad \pi \times r \times r \times \frac{1}{3} \times h \quad = \quad \text{TOTAL VOLUME}$$

sphere formula

cone formula

cube

circle

$$Area = \pi \times r \times r$$

I want pepperoni pizza

First, measure the volume of the cone using the cone formula.

$$\pi \times radius \times radius \times \frac{1}{3} \times height$$

Then measure the ice cream using the sphere formula.

$$radius \times radius \times radius \times \frac{4}{3} \times \pi$$

Once you have the volume of your cone and the volume of your scoop of ice cream, then you just add the two volumes together to measure the whole ice-cream cone.

$$Total\ volume = volume\ of\ cone + volume\ of\ sphere$$

Want to know how much dinner you ate altogether? First, convince your parents to take you out for pizza and ice cream. Then, impress your whole family with how much you've learned about geometry and shapes!

Dark chocolate cake, my favorite!

cylinder

I love nachos!

triangle

$$Area = \frac{1}{2} \times b \times h$$

In order to learn about geometry and shapes and to understand their attributes, you should know about points, lines, and angles!

A **POINT** is represented by a dot.

Lines

A **LINE** extends in two directions and never ends.

RAYS begin at a point and extend out. Two rays together can create an angle.

LINE SEGMENTS make up all the lines in shapes.

PARALLEL LINES never touch, like the yellow lines on a road.

PERPENDICULAR LINES form right angles, like the corner of a book.

INTERSECTING LINES come together to create two obtuse angles and two acute angles.

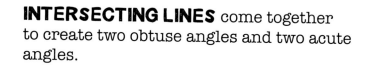

A **VERTEX** is a point where two lines meet to form an angle or the vertex of a figure.

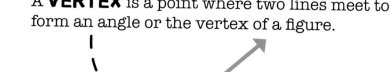

An **ANGLE** is formed by rays that meet at an endpoint. Angles are measured in degrees.

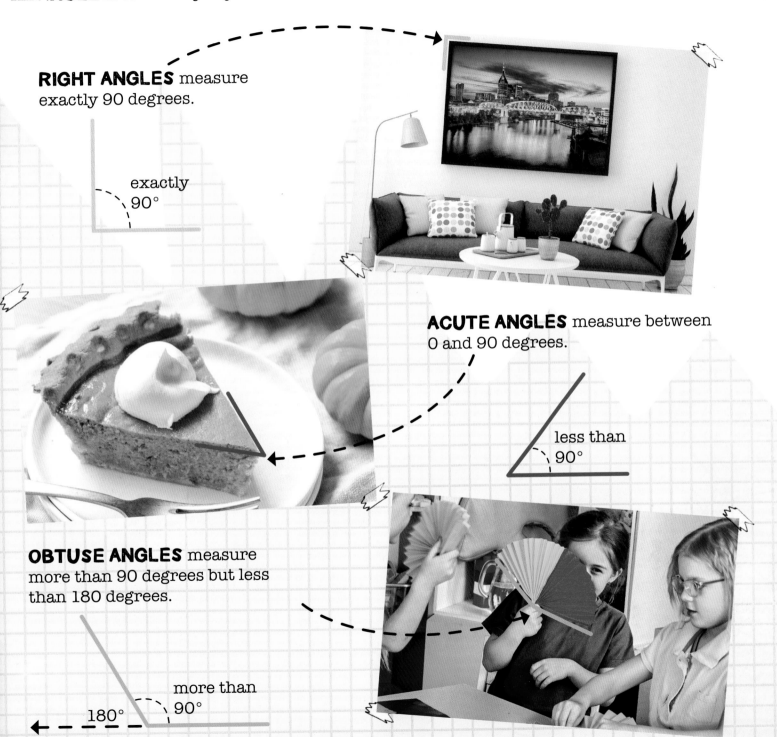

RIGHT ANGLES measure exactly 90 degrees.

exactly 90°

ACUTE ANGLES measure between 0 and 90 degrees.

less than 90°

OBTUSE ANGLES measure more than 90 degrees but less than 180 degrees.

180° more than 90°

There are lots of shapes to learn about in geometry. Each shape, whether it is two-dimensional or three-dimensional, has unique characteristics called attributes that help us tell them apart. Learn about some of the attributes of the shapes below!

TWO-DIMENSIONAL SHAPES are measured in two dimensions: width and length.

CIRCLE

A shape made up of a single curved line that meets at a point.

Sides: 0
Angles: 0

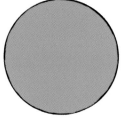

TRIANGLE

A polygon with three straight sides. There are many different types of triangles depending on the degree of their angles.

Sides: 3
Angles: 3

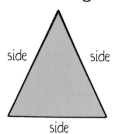

OVAL

A shape similar to a circle. It has a single curved line that creates an egg shape and meets at a point.

Sides: 0
Angles: 0

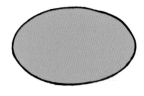

PENTAGON

A polygon with five sides. There can be irregular pentagons with sides that have different lengths or regular pentagons with sides and angles that are all the same.

Sides: 5
Angles: 5

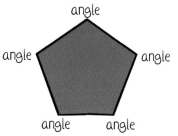

SQUARE

A quadrilateral with sides that are all equal lengths and angles that are all right angles.

Sides: 4
Angles: 4

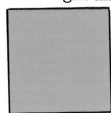

RECTANGLE

A quadrilateral with all right angles, but only its parallel lines are equal lengths.

Sides: 4
Angles: 4

THREE-DIMENSIONAL SHAPES are measured in three dimensions: length, width, and height.

CONE
A figure that has a single face called a base and curved sides that meet at a point.

Faces: 1
Edges: 0
Vertices: 1

SPHERE
A perfectly round figure with all of its outer points equal distance from a center point.

Faces: 0
Edges: 0
Vertices: 0

PYRAMID
A figure with a polygon base and triangular shaped sides that meet at a point.

Faces: 5
Edges: 8
Vertices: 5

vertex
edge
face

CUBE
A figure that has six square faces that are all identical.

Faces: 6
Edges: 12
Vertices: 8

RECTANGULAR PRISM
A figure with six rectangular faces. There can be many types of prisms.

Faces: 6
Edges: 12
Vertices: 8

CYLINDER
A figure with two circular bases.

Faces: 2
Edges: 0
Vertices: 0

GLOSSARY

Acute angle – an angle that measures less than 90 degrees

Angle – a figure measured in degrees formed by two rays that meet at an endpoint

Area – the space occupied by a flat or two-dimensional shape or the surface of an object

Base – the surface a three-dimensional shape stands on or the bottom line of a two-dimensional shape

Circumference – the distance around the outside of a circle

Diameter – the length of a straight line from one side of a circle to the opposite side or from one side of the surface of a sphere to the opposite side

Intersecting lines – lines that come together at a point and form a V shape

Length – the distance from one point to the other of the longer or longest side of a shape

Line – a straight distance that extends into two directions infinitely

Line segment – a part of a line with two endpoints

Obtuse angle – an angle that measures more than 90 degrees but less than 180 degrees

Parallel lines – two lines that never touch

Perpendicular lines – two lines that meet at a point to form a right angle

Pi (π) – the circumference of a circle divided by the diameter

Point – a location represented by a dot that can sometimes be found on a line

Polygon – an enclosed flat figure made up of straight lines

Quadrilateral – a four-sided polygon

Radius – the length of a straight line from the center of a circle or sphere to an outside point of a circle or the surface of a sphere

Ray – a part of a line that starts at a point and extends infinitely

Right angle – an angle that measures exactly 90 degrees

Three-dimensional shape – a solid figure measured in three dimensions: length, width, and height

Two-dimensional shape – a flat shape measured in two dimensions: width and length

Vertex – a point where two or more rays meet

Volume – the space that a three-dimensional shape takes up

Width – the distance measured from one point to the other of a side perpendicular to the side chosen as the length

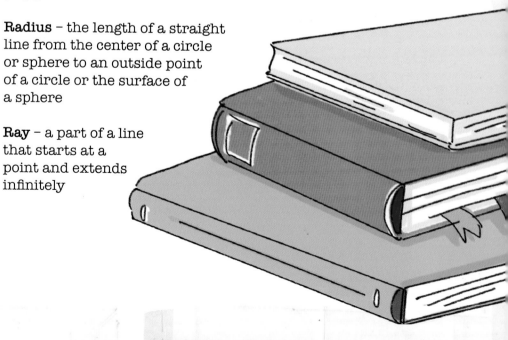